A Note to Parents

DK READERS is a compelling program for beginning readers, designed in conjunction with leading literacy experts, including Dr. Linda Gambrell, Distinguished Professor of Education at Clemson University. Dr. Gambrell has served as President of the National Reading Conference, the College Reading Association, and the International Reading Association.

Beautiful illustrations and superb full-color photographs combine with engaging, easy-to-read stories to offer a fresh approach to each subject in the series. Each DK READER is guaranteed to capture a child's interest while developing his or her reading skills, general knowledge, and love of reading.

The five levels of DK READERS are aimed at different reading abilities, enabling you to choose the books that are exactly right for your child:

Pre-level 1: Learning to read
Level 1: Beginning to read
Level 2: Beginning to read alone
Level 3: Reading alone
Level 4: Proficient readers

The "normal" age at which a child begins to read can be anywhere from three to eight years old. Adult participation through the lower levels is very helpful for providing encouragement, discussing storylines, and sounding out unfamiliar words.

No matter which level you select, you can be sure that you are helping your child learn to read, then read to learn!

LONDON, NEW YORK, MUNICH,
MELBOURNE, and DELHI

For DK/BradyGames

Title Manager Tim Fitzpatrick
Cover Designer Tim Amrhein
Production Designer Wil Cruz
Vice President & Publisher Mike Degler
Editor-In-Chief H. Leigh Davis
Licensing Manager Christian Sumner
Marketing Manager Katie Hemlock
Digital Publishing Manager Tim Cox
Operations Manager Stacey Beheler

Reading Consultant Linda B. Gambrell, Ph.D.

For WWE

Global Publishing Manager Steve Pantaleo
Photo Department Frank Vitucci,
Josh Tottenham, Jamie Nelson, Mike Moran,
JD Sestito, Melissa Halladay, Lea Girard
Legal Lauren Dienes-Middlen

DK/BradyGAMES
800 East 96th St., 3rd floor
Indianapolis, IN 46240

10 9 8 7 6 5 4 3 2

ISBN: 978-1-4654-2297-2 (Paperback)
ISBN: 978-1-4654-2298-9 (Hardback)

Printed in the U.S.A.

The publisher would like to thank the following for their kind
permission to reproduce their photographs:
All photos courtesy WWE Entertainment, Inc.

All other images © Dorling Kindersley
For further information see: www.dkimages.com

Discover more at
www.dk.com

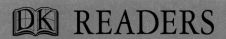

DK READERS

BEGINNING TO READ ALONE

2

Sheamus

Written by Steve Pantaleo

DK

In his young career, Sheamus, nicknamed "The Great White," has taken WWE by storm.

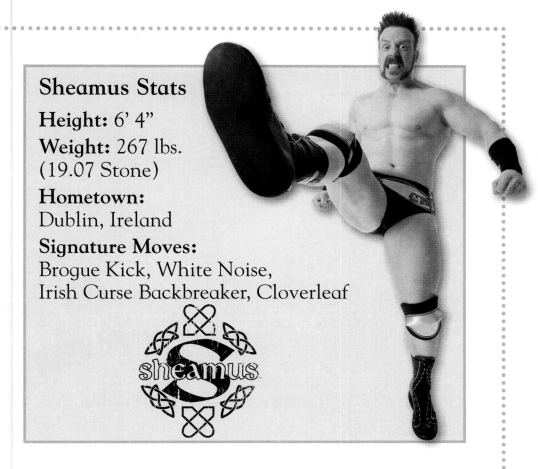

Sheamus Stats

Height: 6' 4"
Weight: 267 lbs.
(19.07 Stone)
Hometown:
Dublin, Ireland
Signature Moves:
Brogue Kick, White Noise,
Irish Curse Backbreaker, Cloverleaf

The first and only Irish-born WWE Champion in history, Sheamus shocked the world by winning the title a mere six months after his WWE debut. For The Celtic Warrior, it was part of a historic quest started centuries ago.

Sheamus descends from a noble bloodline of Celtic warriors. For hundreds of years, the Celts represented the world's most elite fighting force. They were feared all over Europe. Today, Sheamus uses the fierce techniques of his ancestors to flatten opponents inside the ring.

Sheamus first appeared in WWE in June 2009 as part of an effort to bring fresh, new Superstars into the ECW brand. While competing in ECW, he defeated veterans such as Shelton Benjamin and Goldust.

With rippling muscles, milky white skin, and fiery red hair to match his temper, Sheamus stood out from the crowd in ECW. It was not long before he attracted attention from *Monday Night Raw*. In October 2009, he jumped over to WWE's flagship show.

Immediately, Sheamus made his presence felt by pummeling Jamie Noble and announcer Jerry "The King" Lawler. Noble was forced to retire from the damage that Sheamus inflicted. It was clear that this brute Irishman belonged on the big stage.

At *Survivor Series* 2009, Sheamus was a key factor in a five-on-five elimination match. He eliminated two members of the opposition, including team captain John Morrison, to help his team prevail. Sheamus defeated another Irish brawler, Finlay, to earn a spot in a "Breakthrough Battle Royal."

Sheamus Signature Moves

| Brogue Kick | White Noise |

This was set up by Jesse "The Body" Ventura. Any Superstar who had never held a World Championship could enter. A sign of things to come, Sheamus emerged from the crowded pack. The win earned him the right to challenge for the WWE Championship.

Irish Curse Backbreaker

Cloverleaf

Few Superstars in WWE's 50-year history have earned a WWE Championship opportunity in their rookie year. To compound matters, Sheamus would challenge John Cena, WWE's top Superstar. For several years, Cena had dominated WWE. At times, the long-standing champ seemed unbeatable.

Very few people believed that an untested Superstar had a chance against him. Only one man thought Sheamus would win: The Celtic Warrior himself. Sheamus believed that a Tables Match, where the winner is the first to throw his opponent through a table, played right into his hands.

In a battle for the ages, the two competitors collided with force, trading bone-crushing blows. With Sheamus weary and perched on the top turnbuckle, it appeared the reigning champ would drive his opponent through the timber and claim victory. Instead, Sheamus powered out of Cena's grasp and shoved him crashing through the table below. Sheamus stood victorious with his first WWE Championship. His doubters sat in stunned silence, wondering if anyone could stop this uncontrollable Irishman.

Fastest to First WWE Championship

Champion	WWE Debut	First WWE Championship	Days
Pedro Morales*	11/21/70	2/8/71	79
Ric Flair*	9/9/91	1/19/92	132
Yokozuna*	10/31/92	4/4/93	155
Brock Lesnar	3/18/02	8/25/02	160
Sheamus	**6/30/09**	**12/13/09**	**166**
Kane	10/5/97	6/28/98	266
Big Show	2/14/99	11/14/99	273
Kurt Angle	11/14/99	10/22/00	343
Alberto Del Rio	8/20/10	8/14/11	359
Undertaker	11/22/90	11/27/91	370

WWE Hall of Famer

Sheamus was awarded a 2009 Slammy Award for Breakout Superstar of the Year. Although his first reign as WWE Champion was short lived, ending at Elimination Chamber, the Celtic Warrior would not give up.

He quickly turned his attention to the legendary King of Kings, Triple H. The Game would get the best of Sheamus in his first *WrestleMania* match, but he got his revenge weeks later. In a Street Fight at *Extreme Rules*, Sheamus's punishing attacks sidelined Triple H for ten months.

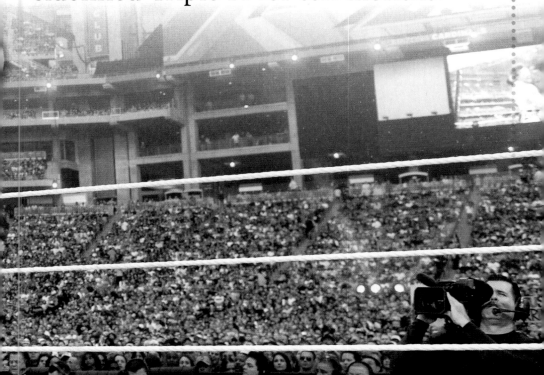

At *Fatal Four Way* in June 2010, Sheamus defeated three top Superstars to reclaim the WWE Championship. Once again, he beat John Cena and won the gold. The merciless bruiser held the title for three months  before losing it in a Six-Pack Challenge Match at *Night of Champions*. Still, The Great White had yet to be defeated in a one-on-one match for the championship.

Hoping to rebound from the setback, Sheamus set his sights on the 2010 *King of the Ring* tournament. With wins against two of WWE's most athletic stars, Kofi Kingston and John Morrison, Sheamus became the 18th King of the Ring in WWE history.

Though most would think it's good to be the king, Sheamus soon faced hardship for the first time.

After more than a year of pushing his fellow Superstars around, Sheamus began to feel the backlash. John Morrison scored a payback win for their *King of the Ring* clash. Then the man he brutally injured ten months earlier, Triple H, inflicted his own brand of punishment on The Great White. Soon, Sheamus found himself on the losing end of matches with the likes of Evan Bourne and future longstanding rival, Daniel Bryan.

When Sheamus was drafted to *SmackDown* in 2011, he seized the opportunity for a fresh start. Seeing the error of his ways,  he shed his bullish nature for a more fan-friendly attitude. Now feeding off the cheers of the WWE Universe, The Great White rattled off a winning streak just in time for the *Royal Rumble*.

The *Royal Rumble* is where the *Road to WrestleMania* begins.

If Sheamus could be the last Superstar remaining after twenty-nine others were tossed from the ring, he would be headed to the Show of Shows.

The match included the 425-pound Big Show and the 2009 winner, Randy Orton. However, the end came down to Sheamus and Chris Jericho. Sheamus used a Brogue Kick to knock Y2J over the top rope.

Epic Championship Triumphs

Fatal Four Way Match for the World Heavyweight Championship
Sheamus vs. Alberto Del Rio vs. Chris Jericho vs. Randy Orton
Over the Limit: May 20, 2012

2-out-of-3 Falls Match for the World Heavyweight Championship
Sheamus vs. Daniel Bryan
Extreme Rules: April 29, 2012

Career vs. United States Title Match
Daniel Bryan vs. Sheamus
Monday Night Raw: March 14, 2011

Steel Cage Match for the WWE Championship
Sheamus vs. John Cena
Money in the Bank: July 18, 2010

Tables Match for the WWE Championship
John Cena vs. Sheamus
WWE TLC: Tables, Ladders & Chairs: December 13, 2009

Just like the Breakthrough Battle Royal two years earlier, the powder-skinned powerhouse was the last man standing when the dust settled on the 2012 *Royal Rumble*.

Two months later at *WrestleMania XXVIII*, Sheamus earned his defining victory in WWE. When Daniel Bryan paused to steal a kiss from bombshell AJ Lee, The Great White capitalized.

Sheamus leveled the distracted "Yes Man" with a Brogue Kick, winning the title match in a record eighteen seconds.

The win kicked off an astounding title reign that cemented Sheamus's status as a dominant force in WWE. One month later, he proved his win over Daniel Bryan was not just luck.

In a 2-out-of-3 Falls Match, Bryan evened the match by snapping on the Yes! Lock. Sheamus was weakened, but not defeated. He summoned all his determination. After surviving an onslaught of kicks from Bryan, the Brogue Kick once again found its mark. Sheamus earned the decisive three-count, winning the grueling match.

As World Heavyweight Champion, Sheamus took on all comers.

He infuriated Alberto Del Rio by taking his prized car for a joyride. The arrogant aristocrat tried everything to take Sheamus's title, even attempting to have the Brogue Kick banned. Still, Sheamus successfully defended the gold against Del Rio, Dolph Ziggler, and others.

When Big Show finally defeated him at *Hell in a Cell* 2012, Sheamus had been champion for 210 days. Since then, he has joined forces with other Superstars to take on The Shield, while

continuing to fight his own battles. He even matched muscle with strongman Mark Henry in a series of strength tests.

Today, Sheamus remains one of the most popular Superstars in WWE. With enough accolades to cement a permanent place in history, his fighting spirit wills him to take on the next challenge. Even after being injured for much of 2013, the Celtic Warrior is back and more aggressive than ever.

Any WWE Superstars on the championship scene had better take notice, because this fella' will always be one Brogue Kick away from a 1-2-3.

Sheamus Facts

- The word "Laoch" on Sheamus's ring attire comes from Ireland's native Gaelic language, and means "warrior" or "hero."

- Sheamus's 210-day reign as World Heavyweight Champion is the third longest in WWE history, behind Triple H and Batista.

- In December 2009, Sheamus lived the dream of several NBA referees by putting Dallas Mavericks owner Mark Cuban through a table.

- In the summer of 2013, Sheamus matched wits with Damien Sandow in a series of intellectual challenges, proving he was more than just brawn.

Index